SOUNDS... IN SESSION

GW00683755

Tyrone Huggins

SOUNDS... IN SESSION

a music theatre piece

Richard

*Hoping that you find
enough in this to
compel you.*

Love

*Tyrone
July 2001*

OBERON BOOKS
LONDON

First published in 1998 by Oberon Books Ltd.

(incorporating Absolute Classics)

521 Caledonian Road, London N7 9RH

Tel: 0171 607 3637 / Fax: 0171 607 3629

e-mail: oberon.books@btinternet.com

British Library Cataloguing-in-Publication-Data
A catalogue record for this book is available from the British Library.

ISBN 1 84002 0962

Cover design: Andrzej Klimowski

Typography: Richard Doust

Printed in Great Britain by Antony Rowe Ltd., Reading.

PREFACE

Sounds In... Session is set in a recording studio during one night as three characters come together to record the final track of a compilation album. Tanya is a young black singer attempting to break free from the 'screeching vocals' that have previously given her chart success. Nic, is a middle-aged white producer, and Tanya's former seducer, who has missed the boat of commercial success – this may be his last chance. Tony is a black man and old school friend of Tanya's, who has resisted being exploited by the music business by keeping his day job, but who has a skill with computer sampled music which the other two need. There is another presence, a computer, driving the most sophisticated music software. Unfortunately it is developing a virus.

Tyrone Huggins
London 1998

Acknowledgements

Sounds... In Session has allowed *Theatre of Darkness* to form itself as an amalgam of multi-disciplined artists. These include Carol Pemberton, founder and Music Director of *Black Voices* utilising her skills as Administrator. Ruth Nutter, Producer for *The People Show* operating as Marketing Director. Norman Bailey, Theatre Hand and Installation Artist working as Assistant Director. Tony Graves, Producer carrying out the role of Producer. Rebecca Child and Kelly Eldridge, as placement students, filling many gaps. Aaron Mapp, Technical Co-ordination. Katie Branigan, Dramaturg. All working on a complex, chaotic, process-based theatre piece. What luxury.

Characters

NIC FORCAST

middle aged, male, white. He once owned an *indie* label, before selling out to a mega-bucks commercial label reduced him to producing cheesy disco hits. He needs the credibility of a commercial hit if he's to escape being a has-been

TONY HAMILTON

young, male, black – is a social worker by day. At night in his bedroom he unlocks inspiration from his computer-based sound system, creating music in the ether that nobody hears. This is his first exposure to the manipulative world of the biz

TANYA GEORGE

young, female, black, was a two hit wonder in the early nineties with *hi-NRG* versions of sixties hits. Time, and artistic introspection, have transformed her, now she is ready to seize control and steer the direction of her career in the music biz

Sounds... In Session was first performed by *Theatre Of Darkness* at The Viaduct Theatre, Halifax on the 10th of November 1998, transferring to the Hackney Empire, London on the 25th November 1998. The cast was as follows:

NIC FORCAST, Graeme Rose

TONY HAMILTON, Michael Aduwali

TANYA GEORGE, Michelle Joseph

Director, Tyrone Huggins

Musicians/Composers, Gladstone Wilson, Alex Searle

Designer, Kendra Ullyart

Note:
All sound references are contained on computer annotated version of script, (Macintosh format). All enquiries to Tim Scott Personal Management.

Track 1

Home At Last

The soundscape setting is a basement recording studio, located somewhere. A possible location for this shop would be in a run down parade away from main thoroughfares, probably near open ground, such as a park, or cemetery. The recording studio is in darkness. We can just hear, in the street outside; traffic passing at a distance; dogs barking; a car alarm singing at top pitch. Mixed into this soundscape, also at a distance, is the voice of a man shrieking out a phrase marked in a slow metronomic tempo; "call the police!" – this will persist throughout Track 1. Sound reference. When the soundscape has been fully established we hear a door opening.

NIC: I made the mistake of coming through the city, traffic was murder. There was this guy I had to meet at this album launch, didn't arrive till late. What could I do. I had to stay. Let's shed some light. Oh, no lights... you been waiting long?

TONY: I was early.

NIC: What's the time now?

TONY: I can't see.

NIC: Oh yeah, right. Must have gone half midnight. Could do with some light.

TONY: I got a torch in my car.

NIC: Great. OK.

TONY exits.

Right. That's the door. I know this place like the inside of my eyelids. Ouch! Dammit Dave, you could have left it set up for me.

TONY returns.

TONY: You in here?

NIC: Yeah. Got that torch?

TONY: Yeah.

NIC: Ta. Ah. A Maglight! The professional's third eye. May the Force be with you! Saviour in the belt-clip of many a black-clad engineer. Somewhere round here, in this tangle of wires is...

NIC feels for and trips the light switch. A light in the sound booth comes on.

Ah.

TONY: Smells damp in here.

NIC: Just needs a little airing.

TONY: Got to lock my car. And get the rest of my stuff in.

NIC: Yeah, I would round here! I mean its not bad, but its not good. Its not safe anywhere.

TONY: Will it be alright out there.

NIC: Yeah sure, its not that bad.

TONY: Right.

TONY exits.

NIC: Dave, you really have let your anarchy run this place haven't you. I hope to heaven this gear works.

NIC throws a switch which brings the sound equipment to life. There is a stack of sound processing equipment, surmounted by an old four track tape recorder. He surveys the room with a hint of despair. TONY returns.

By the way, I'm Nic. (*Extends hand.*)

TONY: From the phone call. Tony.

NIC: I know we know who we are, but I like to conclude the formalities. Can I give you a hand?

TONY: It's OK, it's all in now.

NIC: Oh. Is that the lot? Well, its nice and compact. Tanya hates being early, so arrives deliberately late. She is such a Diva.

TONY: Well, I got to set up.

NIC: Yeah, I was at this industry bash. Album launch – *Boyz R Us* – heard of them? Clones of *Sell This* and all the other manufactured bands that come and go. Pre-pubescent-babe bait. Packaged to squeeze cream from the sweet-teens into the coffers. Gleaming teeth, pelvic thrusts and the promise of later, you know the story. Nothing to do with music.

TONY: I was wondering where I should set up?

NIC: I mean that is so easy. I could do that stuff. I got jammed in this seat next to this model type wannabee, couldn't have been more than nineteen, seventeen – how can you tell. I told her I was a producer and she was practically eating out of my lap. I was sorely tempted. But I thought, I'm in the studio tonight. My destiny is waiting.

TONY: Is there any more light?

NIC: The Mains Breaker is over there, have a look.

TONY: Have you finished with the torch?

NIC: Oh yeah, sorry. Take it.

TONY: This isn't your studio then?

NIC: No, but I know it well. Helped to set it up nearly... yeah nearly fifteen years ago now. Belongs to my mate Dave. Started my own label here. White Line Records. Had a few good bands.

TONY: This wiring looks a bit dodgy to me.

NIC: *Revolt*? Heard of them?

TONY: No.

NIC: *Crash The System* got to number ten in Holland. *Fools For Fashion*, they were the big one. Then there was Tanya. Signed her six years ago.

TONY: Was that you?

NIC: Yeah. You heard of me?

TONY: No. It's just that was the time I lost touch with Tanya.

NIC: Oh.

TONY: When she had those hits.

NIC: I was her Producer.

TONY: You were producer on those?

NIC: Yup. Two number ones.

TONY: Right. The power's on but not much more light.

NIC: I'll sort that out. Met this executive Simon tonight. Soon as I mentioned I was going into the studio with Tanya George, his eyes lit up. I thought yeah. If you want her you're gonna have to come through me.

TONY: Could you hold this torch, I can't see what I'm doing.

NIC: Oh yeah, sure. He's flying off to Florida this afternoon, so we're on a bit of a timetable. I'll get you some proper light.

TONY: That would be useful.

There is a time slip.

NIC: So, you known Tanya long.

TONY: Since time. We grew up together.

NIC: Oh right, school and that?

TONY: Yeah. School, nursery, church.

NIC: But you missed her chart topping years?

TONY: Don't know that I missed that much.

NIC: You're a musician then?

TONY: I make music, but I wouldn't call myself a musician, no.

NIC: Well I need more of an engineer than a musician for this ghoster.

TONY: I'm not an engineer.

NIC: Sorry? You're not an engineer?

TONY: No.

NIC: So what are you here for?

TONY: Tanya asked me to come down.

NIC: Right. And you're not a musician?

TONY: No. Well sort of, my instrument is the computer.

NIC: But you got all the gear, samplers, keyboards, effects – digital stuff.

TONY: Inside my computer.

NIC: And you know how to operate it.

TONY: Yeah.

NIC: That's alright then.

TONY: What's wanted?

NIC: Demo quality music. Not virtual reality.

TONY: Demo?

NIC: In demo world music is more than just making squiggly sounds. It's Rock and Roll, it's Blues, it's Jazz, Soul, R&B, Classical – it's popular music – real life! I used to be a roadie. When being on the road was the back of a freezing Transit, with the hi-hat stand poking up your arse. Played a gig in Brodies Bar, Edinburgh, really stomping night. De-rigged, loaded up got some beers in to take to the flat. The band got there first, of course, taken all the beds. The sound engineer and me were left with sleeping bags on the floor – they get the glamour, we get the crick in the neck. Just got off to sleep when Susie, the singer, came running in, shrieking – just like she sang – "there's a man killing a woman out on the streets!" As if it was any of my business. Half asleep dragged my jeans on – no shoes – ran down five flights of stairs out the front of that tenement to see this couple. Man's got hold of her face, she's got his hair scratching like a vixen yelling murder at each other; "why don't you kill me then go on kill me why don't you kill me!" She's shouting over and over. And he's shouting, "shut up, shut up... you want me to kill you, shut up!" And I'm witnessing this, "why don't you kill me!" And I say hang on, cool it

you two, cool it, let her go mate, or something
equally foolish. Next thing I know he's turned on
me. "Who the fuck are you? What the fuck's it
got to do with you?" And he lets her go. Splat!
Right on the nose. Blood. Like Rocky. Then she's
coming scratching and kicking and screaming, at
me now. In a daze, blood on me Buzzcocks tee
shirt, I stumble back to the door of the block.
I've locked myself out. There's an array of door-
bells swimming out of focus in front of me –
I don't know which flat we're in! In me bare feet,
freezing. (*Pause.*) After waking half the block
I get back inside, they're carrying on; "why don't
you kill me then go on kill me!" Susie's back in
bed, fast asleep. Life, as lived by real people.
I learned about passion that night. (*Pause.*) Never
come between other people's passion.

TONY: Seen any phono leads?

NIC: Should be a pile down there. Why's it so dark
in here?

*NIC hunts about trying switches until light begins to fill the room
and it becomes clearly visible for the first time.*

That's better. Now I can see myself think.

TONY: I'm just about set up.

NIC: Let's get some sounds going. (*Loading a cassette.*)
Shit, nothing coming through. Dave, don't let me
down now.

TONY: I can see why its called Twilight Studios.

NIC: It's dead. There's nothing coming through.

TONY: Where's the amp?

NIC: Down here. Its on.

TONY: Where's that go to.

NIC: I dunno, cables everywhere.

TONY: Spaghetti. That's one thing you don't get with my system. You get spam instead.

NIC: Why is nothing coming through?

TONY: Hang on. What's this? This could do with one serious clean.

TONY unplugs and plugs, until eventually **Track 1** *is heard. Sound reference. NIC takes over the controls.*

NIC: Great! Listen to this. Cute eh?

TONY: If you like that sort of thing.

NIC: My mate Paul's gone over to producing classical. There's money in heritage. Kinda snuggley innit.

TONY: Kinda sick making.

NIC: That's a bit harsh.

TONY: Listening to this, I imagine pink cheeked, cherub faced privileged kids, in stone-ancient churches and green and pleasant lawns. Imagine in-bred Lord somebody reaping a few million more from third world commodities he's selling back to the third world.

NIC: You what? Oh dear.

TONY: Yeah, oh dear.

NIC: That's politics. This is an innocent piece of music. I mean they're not singing about oppressing black people, are they? Be fair.

TONY: True. But music isn't innocent, it's fundamental communication. Whatever. I can never imagine any black cherubs, that's what I don't like.

NIC: OK. I like it.

NIC rewinds and replays the cassette.

You could feed all the samples into any machine you like, it could never produce anything like this.

TONY: And that's what you call making music?

There is cross-fade effect as we begin to hear music from the system. Sound reference, **Track 2, Tony's Tune**, *which TONY will balance and equalise at the mixer on his computer screen.*

No, it's what I call manipulating sound.

NIC: Is this as good as it gets?

Track 2

Tony's Tune

TONY is preoccupied with adjusting the sound balance on **Track 2.**

TONY: It's not EQ-ing properly. It should sound better than this.

NIC: Yeah.

TONY: It's lyricism played out within a dynamic. You'd have to hear it all.

NIC: This is just chill out music isn't it? It's not gonna get the masses dancing in the street, or buying Levi's.

TONY: It's not intended to.

TONY stands and moves around the room, intently listening to the sound. There is a time slip.

I'm sorry its system, is Jurassic. There's no separation in the highs. And can you hear that hum? There's a bad earth somewhere.

NIC: It's the place where technology has taken control.

TONY: (*Inspecting mixer.*) Analogue equaliser. I thought these were washed away with the ark. With this tune, the high's should be right up there. The mid-bass here. And the sub-bass like an earthquake rumble. These speakers can't handle it.

NIC: I once had a neighbour who liked his reggae up loud. *The Stranglers* soon silenced him.

TONY: These capacitors are drawing their pensions. Listen to that rumble and that hiss.

NIC: Raw music doesn't worry about the detail.

TONY: I can't listen to this.

NIC: The more delicate this equipment gets, the less life comes out in the music.

TONY: It's the mixer. I'll have to by-pass it. Go straight out of the DB-2 into the power amp. See if that's better.

NIC: Look mate, don't worry about it.

TONY: I just want to see if I can't tweak up the signal by using the mixer in the software. Set-up like this it takes eight midi channels out from the DB-2; translated by the midi converter, half heard by that mixer, conducted through an unsound hard-wired network, through over-worked pots and retired transistors – I wouldn't be surprised to find fossilised valves in there – picking up noise all the way, through to those fagged out faders, increasingly distorted by isolated contacts, enfeebled masters, emerging, presumably in stereo, though possibly... switched to send on A to those decrepit sound confusers and squeezed out onto four tracks of metal oxide silverfish floating in a plastic sea, read by heads pitted like B roads and supposed to represent music! All the way creativity picks up noise, and signals are attenuated by everything from burnt out components, to bits of chicken tikka that've worked their way into the circuitry. And if that isn't bad enough, the biggest loss is gained by transferring solid state signals generated in mu amps from my system, to this pile of junk. I'm sorry to dis this studio, but it's rubbish.

TONY stops **Track 2** *on the computer.*

NIC: Now you're talking like an engineer. That's good. So how are you going to sort it out so we can work.

TONY: Like I said.

NIC: Niké.

TONY: Huh?

NIC: Niké – 'Just do it'. I'm not a trainspotter, I'm not interested in what goes on inside these machines.

NIC: I used to enjoy techie talk – excuse me sounding like my old man – but in my day, if the technology didn't work, a bloody good kick would sort it out. You just get the best sound you can, I'll get the best demo.

TONY: My home studio is better than this.

NIC: Well, we're here now. So get tweaking.

TONY sets about re-patching the system. NIC loads a quarter inch spool onto the tape deck. The soundscape continues as there is a time slip.

(*Opening vodka.*) Want some?

TONY: I don't.

NIC: C'mon, get you in the mood.

TONY: No thanks.

NIC: It's going to be a long night.

TONY: No, thank you.

NIC: You'd never survive in the music industry. There's only one or two I know who've got anywhere by not drinking. They are usually the ones into meditation and tantric sex. You see ours is a social profession. Got to be able to get on with people – socially.

TONY: I just don't drink that's all.

NIC: Fair enough. You are an outsider. I know people who've reformed. Alcohol, drugs, whatever. That's OK, they've sold their soul for Rock and Roll.

TONY: Isn't it their health they're selling.

NIC: But if you start off your way, totally clean. That way lies death – of your career. You're boring. And that's the worst thing you could ever be in this business. Might as well be Cliff Richard and have done. Some great boozers, had some wild nights. Not stopped at alcohol neither.

TONY: That should be it. Do a lot of gigs then?

TONY starts **Track 2** *from the computer.*

NIC: No computers then. It was heavy shit. Marshall's were the dogs. Drop one of those amps, go straight through the floor, and still come up rocking. Simple too. One light, on: no lights, off. None of this flashing digital rainbow coloured double the price rip-off bullshit.

TONY: Doesn't sound like my idea of fun.

NIC: Biggest problem ever was changing a red hot valve in the middle of a gig.

TONY: (*Holding up disc.*) Couldn't put it in your pocket.

NIC: Didn't want to either. Nor on our laps. Feedback, volume, reverb was all you needed to know. No micro this and mega-giga that.

TONY: Sounds... simple.

NIC: Oh it was. Meant you could concentrate on making music. Real music.

TONY: I can get any type of music out of my machine.

NIC: I mean I'm not out of touch, but what's happened to hands-on involvement in things. Don't people matter any more?

TONY: Its become the finger on the screen. Accessible to more people.

NIC: Yeah, but we went out and played gigs in front of people. Now it's people sitting alone in their bedrooms. Look at it this way, real people are under attack, from computers on one hand, and bloody accountants on the other. We're all being made redundant.

TONY: Unless you're computer literate.

NIC: Not me. Getting square-eyed in front of a TV, where's the meaning in that? It's bad enough you can't sell a record without a poxy video. I'm not turning my job into a virtual relationship with the ether world. I'm good with artists. That's what I'm good at. Getting them to give more than they thought they had. Blending music and inspiration.

TONY: There's a world behind this screen that you don't know until you've been there. And it can't be imagined. That's the two systems grafted together. Sounds better. State of the art controlling state of the ark.

"Call the police..." once more becomes pervasive. There is a time slip.

NIC: What's the time now?

TONY: Nearly ten past one.

NIC: I'm beginning to worry. Tanya's usually late, but not this late. And that character out there's been sounding off all of my lifetime. Where are the police when madmen are wandering the streets?

TONY: Harassing the innocent and the purposeless.

NIC: You see, that's what I like about those cherubs singing that song. It's peaceful, tranquil, lyrical.

TONY: It's not the real world. It never was.

NIC: There's too much mess in the real world. (*Decisive.*) I'm going to check out that loony!

TONY: I saw him earlier. While I was waiting. He's in the park across the road. Standing there in the dark. Calling to keep himself company. He's safe. Just doing his community service.

NIC: I wish he was safely behind bars! Where is Tanya?

TONY: Give her a call.

NIC: No phone here.

TONY: I've got my mobile.

NIC: Of course you have.

TONY digs in his bag and finds his mobile phone.

Do you have her number?

TONY: Hang on... it's in Memory.

NIC: Who needs to think?

TONY finds and dials the number.

Track 3

Tanya's Message

A new sound will begin slowly to creep into the present soundscape, mixing into the external soundscape subsuming the track presently playing on the Teac. It is the music that Tanya is presently listening to on her walkman **Track 3; Tanya's Message.** *Sound reference. By it's peak, Track 3 will have climbed in volume till it is standing above the mix of the other tracks and voices. The following dialogue sequence will then have to wrestle with it for communication.*

TONY: It's ringing. (*Listens then shakes head.*) Answerphone!

NIC: Give it here?

With this he takes the phone and listens. TONY returns to his experimentation with the system, whilst remaining attentive to NIC. We hear TANYA's voice announcing from her answerphone. It is backed with music.

TANYA: (*Voice over.*) Hi I'm not here. Leave me a message or call back when I'm in. (*Beep.*)

NIC: (*Into phone.*) Tanya? If you're there, answer the phone... it's Nic... it's after one now and I'm beginning to wonder where you are... if you are there pick up the phone and let me know that you're alright. I'm here with Tony on his mobile. And the number is... (*A look at TONY.*)

TONY: 0-9-7-3...

NIC: 0-9-7-3...

TONY: 8-8-3...

NIC: 8-8-3...

TONY: 6-3-4.

NIC: 6-3-4. So if you get this message call us here.

Buzzer.

TONY: Did you hear something?

NIC: No. (*Listening to phone.*) Nothing... she's not there. Maybe she's left a message on my answering machine.

TONY: Everything's connected.

NIC: How do I dial?

TONY: Dial the number. Then press the green one. (*Indicating.*)

As NIC dials his home TONY adjusts **Track 2**, *playing from the computer. Sound reference.*

NIC: I'm through.

We hear NIC's voice announcing from his answerphone.

(*Voice over.*) You've reached Nicholas Forcast and I'm not here right now, please leave your name and telephone number and the time that you called so I can get back to you. (*Beep.*)

A buzzer sounds.

TONY: There! I did hear something!

NIC: (*Looking at phone.*) No it's my answering machine
– Oh! I've forgot my bleeper – I can't get the
messages back.

Buzzer.

TONY: Listen.

NIC: What?

TONY: I'm sure I heard a buzzer.

NIC: I can't tell one bleep from another.

TONY: Look!

*TONY indicates an intercom hanging beside the door. Its buzzer
sounds good and long.*

There!

*NIC goes to pick up the intercom. We then hear the intercom
conversation mixed into the present sound balance.*

NIC: Hello? (*Thrusting mobile.*) Here take this.
Hello? Is that you Tanya?

TANYA: Nic!

NIC: Tanya! We're in the basement.

TANYA: I can hardly hear you Nic!

NIC: (*Shouting.*) We're in the basement! Down the
stairs to your right! I'll buzz you in!

TANYA: Bin? What bin?

NIC: I said... I'll buzz-you-in! Tony, cut that noise!

TONY stops the computer, then the Teac, leaving **Track 3** *in the
ascendancy.*

TANYA: How do I get in Nic!

NIC: (*Into receiver.*) Tanya!

TANYA: I can't see a door!

NIC: The door... is-down-the-stairs... to your right!

TONY: I'll get her.

With that, TONY exits the room.

TANYA: It's pitch black Nic! I can't see anything. Put some light on!

NIC: Tony's coming out!

TANYA: There's a man coming Nic! Nic there's a man coming!

TONY: Tanya!

TANYA: What d'you want!

NIC: Tanya?

TONY: It's me. Tony. Tanya come back!

TANYA: Tony? Tony! Jesus Tony! You frightened me half to death man!

TONY: We're in the basement.

TANYA: You frightened me half to death... it's terrifying here...

At this the voices go 'off mike', though the soundscape remains present in this form till NIC hangs up. NIC hangs up the intercom. **Track 3** *continues to grow in volume, peaking when TANYA enters. Meanwhile NIC wanders over to the computer to examine the images on it's VDU. He is in this mode, when TANYA enters ahead of TONY. She is wearing headphones and is agitated.*

... I've been up and down the street for the last half hour. I had to get a taxi. My car wouldn't start. I called the AA and even though I told them I was a woman on my own they said they wouldn't get there for an hour. Suppose it was an emergency!

NIC: Tanya, you're here now.

TANYA: And I called a taxi and they said they'd be five minutes... I waited half an hour! That's the last time I use them –

NIC: You're here now Tanya.

TANYA: And the driver – this really vexed me man – pulls up down the other end of the street – I told him to wait – and he drives off! So I'm left in the middle of nowhere! I didn't know where in hell I was! I could have been killed for all he cared!

TONY: That's terrible.

NIC: You're here now. Do you want a drink?

TANYA: I mean what kind of man would do a thing like that?

TONY: Especially around here.

NIC: Tanya, is your walkman on?

TANYA: What?

NIC: Is your walkman on? You're shouting.

TANYA: Of course I'm shouting. I'm still shaking, feel my hand.

NIC: (*Calmly taking hand.*) Tanya, turn the music off!

TANYA: It was terrifying out there!

NIC: Tanya. You can't hear yourself think – you're shouting!

TANYA: Where the hell is this place! Why didn't you tell me you were bringing me to the end of the world!

NIC: (*Shouting.*) Tanya!

TANYA: (*Halted.*) What!

NIC: (*Miming earphone.*) Turn off the music!

> *NIC grabs her walkman, switching it off.* **Track 3 cuts**. *There is now silence for the first time. NIC puts his head in his hands and slumps into the sofa.*

Thank God. (*Quietly.*) There. Tanya. Isn't that better? Tranquillity?

TANYA: (*Taking off again.*) I'm serious Nic! Look at me I'm quivering. This isn't funny.

NIC: I'm not laughing.

TANYA: You don't know what it's like. There were cars slowing down like I was a prostitute. And there's some crazy guy in that cemetery across the road, howling like he's ready for his next victim. "Call the police," to inspect my dead body. I had to turn my music up to block out the sound of him killing me!

> *This thought strikes her, bringing her close to tears. NIC moves to comfort her.*

NIC: It's OK, I'm sorry. Look, I should have picked you up or something – I don't know. I didn't think.

TANYA: I didn't know where I was supposed to go. I thought I was going to die.

TONY: Do you want a cup of tea, or something.

NIC: That's right, a drink. Have some vodka, you'll feel better.

TANYA: I don't want alcohol. I don't drink.

NIC: Since when?

TANYA: Over a year now.

NIC: Oh. I've got some Charley, if you prefer?

TANYA looks at NIC, who looks at TONY, who looks at TANYA.

TANYA: No thanks. I've brought some herbal tea.

TONY: I'll see if there's a kettle.

TANYA: Leave the bag in Tony, I don't like it weak.

TONY: (*To NIC.*) Do you?

NIC: (*Brandishing vodka.*) I wouldn't mind a glass.

TONY: Sure.

TANYA: Thanks Tony.

TONY: No probs. (*Exits.*)

There is a hiatus.

TANYA: What's that smell. This is a place where germs come to catch germs.

NIC: Antiseptic. (*Swigs.*)

TANYA: This is the middle of nowhere. I know you said it wasn't Abbey Road, but I wasn't expecting the Black Hole of Calcutta.

NIC: It's the best I could get for nothing.

TANYA: Does anyone use this place?

NIC: This is where I started White Line. My bands used to use it a lot.

TANYA: They were all punk bands, they're used to crap.

NIC: We won't have to come back to anything like this, I promise.

TANYA: Don't promise anything Nic, you can't deliver.

NIC: No really, this time. You remember that guy at Bully Boys, Simon –

TANYA: Simon? The smarmy one?

NIC: – he's really interested. I said I'd drop in to see him this morning.

TANYA: What for?

NIC: He's off to Florida this afternoon –

TANYA: So?

NIC: Well, it was open door when I said I was seeing you.

TANYA: Nic, what are you driving at?

NIC: I thought, if I could drop off a demo –

TANYA: You thought?

NIC: I told him I'd have a demo for him...

TANYA: When?

NIC: In the morning.

TANYA: Oh Nic!

NIC: It's OK I –

TANYA: Why did you do that Nic?

NIC: To be honest Tanya, I thought there was no point going in there empty handed.

TANYA: That's not what I want.

NIC: Yeah I know. Just a little fire under the frying pan.

TANYA: I don't want to get mixed up with record companies. Not yet. Not till I know what I'm doing.

NIC: Yeah, and I realise that, but studio time costs. This way we might get... we got a stronger possibility of... next time we'll get something better than this. Things have changed there, they got a bigger A & R budget. The industry is crying out for something new, and we've done half the work already. On these tapes.

TANYA: And how are we supposed to produce a demo in this place?

NIC: Well, we got the tapes and your friend, Tony, has his computer.

TANYA: And that's another thing. I only got Tony involved cos he's not interested in the industry.

NIC: And that was a really great idea of yours. I had all our material digitised. He'll be able to reproduce it at the click of a button.

TANYA: I'm not getting Tony involved in all that crap. Oh Nic, you've messed up again.

NIC: No Tanya, I'm not taking this. You asked me to help you. After eighteen months of not hearing a word from you. Not even "how are you Nic, how're you doing?" And when I help you the way I know how, you say I've messed up. Well I don't see it that way. I'm trying to help us both. And if you don't like it...

TONY enters.

TONY: You don't want sugar do you?

TANYA: No, thanks Tony.

TONY: And there's no milk.

TANYA: Only a pleb would put milk in herb tea.

TONY: I'm a pleb. That Kettle's boiling in slow motion, wont be long now. (*Leaves.*)

TANYA: You're right. I shouldn't have got you involved.

NIC: No Tanya, I want to be involved in everything you do. I want to help you.

TANYA: I don't want what we had before. I know myself better. I've grown up.

NIC: We both have.

TANYA: Back then I thought getting into the charts and on Top of the Pops was my passport out of mundane, depressing, reality. But it got out of control. Remember my tantrums, when we were working on that third single? That wasn't me. I felt trapped. Sex, Vodka, Cocaine. One, two, then ten lines a day. Why not, it numbed the sensation of damage. But my soul was being eaten by it, everyone helping themselves to a piece of me. I don't want anyone to help me anymore. I want to help myself.

NIC: You saying you were prostituting yourself?

TANYA: What they never ask about prostitution is; is it worth the price? To begin with it was, by the end, no.

NIC: We all pay a price. I lost my label over you.

TANYA: Nic, you can't put that one on me.

NIC: To begin with it was worth it. By the end, it nearly really was worth it. You are the only one that ever came close to unique. But when things got rough you beat the retreat, the drawbridge went up, and I was left holding... nothing.

TANYA: I'm sorry about all that Nic...

TONY re-enters with tea.

TONY: There you go.

TANYA: Thanks.

NIC: Was there a glass?

TONY: Yeah, sorry I –

NIC: I'll get it. I won't get another opportunity like this Tanya. Everything I've touched since you has crumbled into dust.

TANYA: White powder? This may look like a chance for you Nic, but I left the battlefield early because there's no point in scrabbling around for every half chance going. You only end up with the scraps that way.

NIC: Meaning?

TANYA: Meaning I'm not doing this, in the hope that some uninspired executive will decide that I'm the next best thing since the last best thing. I have to look after my soul. My spirit. I'm after existential permanence, staying power. I'm taking my music deadly serious. Because it's an expression of me. Look at this place Nic, it's amateur. All this place is saying to me is... die. Stay in the cesspit and die. If the music I make isn't worth better than this, it won't ever be better than this. I can't even drink out of this cup. That's how I feel.

NIC exits to kitchen. TONY, aware of the atmosphere, crosses to his bag, pulls out a can of coke.

TONY: Right. What's the plan?

TANYA: Tony, thanks for coming down to help me out like this, how are you doing? –

TONY: No probs.

TANYA: I think I might have made a mistake getting you involved in this.

TONY: Involved? In what? I haven't done anything yet.

TANYA: I'm sorry we haven't had a chance to talk about things properly.

TONY: That's OK, I'm easy.

TANYA: I've just been talking to Nic, and I realise now that I got two different ideas confused into one.

TONY: Mm.

TANYA: Nic and I had been working on an album a couple of years ago, I was planning a change in musical direction. I got stuck about what to do, then your tape arrived.

TONY: I wasn't expecting anything out of it, if that's what you're worried about.

TANYA: No, I know. As soon as it arrived I was inspired. But now I've arrived in this place I can feel my energy draining away.

TONY: That's what black holes do.

TANYA: So I'm thinking we should call tonight off.

TONY: (*Nodding head.*) 'S cool. D'you want to arrange it for another time. To be honest I haven't felt a good vibe. We could get together at my flat any time.

TANYA: Sure. That'd be good. I don't feel like I could sing tonight anyway. I feel like I've lost my voice.

TONY: You've always had a voice. You've sung since we were kids. Confidence, the right environment, that's all you need.

TONY makes first moves towards packing up. He gazes at his computer screen.

TONY: I was looking forward to this. Me and you playing around with music. You get too introspective on your own. I do anyway. My music's going nowhere.

NIC enters during this.

TANYA: It is. It is going somewhere. That's what I'm saying. It was hearing what you were getting out of your machine. It was deep and emotional. I think I've lost that. Maybe Nic's right. I should re-launch my career. But what for? I can't think of anything to say with my music.

NIC: Tanya there wasn't 'your' music when you started. All you had was a voice. I found all your material. I arranged it. I styled you.

TANYA: I was there remember! That's what I'm saying. I was miming. I don't have anything to say. So I mime the meaning.

NIC: And it's all down to how you've been exploited right?

TANYA: Turn off that record Nic, it's worn out!

NIC: You know it strikes me that there are a few other exploited species on the planet. Like the people who help people. The people who actually make an effort to create opportunities – to help their friends. I know people crying out for the opportunities you've had, to be the next best thing since the last best thing. I lost all I had trying to help you find your voice.

TANYA: I didn't ask you to Nic.

NIC: Didn't you? I thought we cared for each other. Look at me. I'm finished. In eight hours I've got one chance. All I need is your voice, on a demo. And you choose right now to lose it? I could get us all out of this shit-hole. If someone just believed in me. I have to have some air.

NIC collects his vodka and exits. TONY sits at his computer and begins to operate it.

Track 4

Reunion

*Out of his play, TONY sets up a metronomic, bass based, loop which will repeat itself at intervals throughout this scene **Track** 4. He takes a glance at TANYA, who is staring into an inner world. Then, scrimmaging in his bag he finds a packet of ten silk cut, out of which he draws a pre-rolled spliff, which he lights up, inhales on deeply, before offering it to TANYA. She refuses it.*

TANYA: No. I'm off it.

TONY: (*Nodding to himself.*) Never knew you were on to it. Couldn't imagine you drawing on a spliff. Not Tanya.

TANYA: Imagine it. I've done it. Seen the story, heard the book lived the film. Been there. Long way from home.

TONY: Too far to go back?

TANYA: Yeah. And I don't remember it being so wonderful anyway.

TONY: There were good things. We were all innocent then, weren't we? Kids. I used to think everything was going to be easy.

TANYA: That's the point of being a kid. Everything is easy. You just don't see the strain on adult's faces. Problem is, it don't prepare you for that strain, when innocence turns into responsibility.

TONY: So where do we start?

TANYA: Start?

TONY: To get prepared. To catch up.

TANYA: Oh, you don't want to. I don't want to.

TONY: It's been a long time.

TANYA: Yeah. Look, Tony, I'm sorry about –

TONY: You want to lighten up, you know.

TANYA: Do I?

TONY: Yeah. You've become so intense. You're gonna spontaneously combust soon.

TANYA: I don't feel like it. I feel cold inside.

TONY: It's called frustration. "It's a black thang". Remember that game 'hot and cold'?

TANYA: No.

TONY: Yes you do. We used to play it.

TANYA: I don't remember. How?

TONY: You start off at the ankle, and work your way up the leg, saying 'hot?', or 'cold?'.

TANYA: Don't remember that. Must have been in your dreams.

TONY: No. We used to play it. Group of us.

TANYA: Definitely not me.

TONY: Yes. You played it. Didn't think you would, but you loved it. Was the only time you ever did anything wrong.

TANYA: You seem to have this picture of me as some kind of pure virgin.

TONY: I wouldn't have said virgin. I don't know what you got up to on that front. But you were a 'good girl'.

TANYA: No. You don't know what went on inside my head. It was pure wickedness.

TONY: Wish I had known.

TANYA: No, it wasn't that exciting. I always felt like I had to be two different people.

TONY: Mm?

TANYA: The person for the people around me, and the person for me.

TONY: What's the difference?

TANYA: One was the person everyone saw, hard working and conforming. But the me I knew, had dreams and visions. For a long time I thought I was a witch. One time my mom said I was an Obeah woman. Now I know that I am.

TONY: How do you know?

TANYA: I can speak to and read other peoples minds. I'm telepathic.

TONY: I bet you don't know what I'm thinking now.

TANYA: Yes I do and you can put that thought back in your trousers.

TONY: (*A laugh that builds.*) Yeah, good. That's good.

TANYA: It's not true.

TONY: I understand now why I've carried this thing about you, like nobody else, and I don't mean I want to draw down your panties – which I do – but, I know you. I know that side of you that you try to keep to yourself. You've spent your lifetime trying to hide what was impossible to hide. You are an Obeah woman. (*Laughs.*) That's so funny.

TANYA: Look at you giggling like a baby. That's the weed man, that's the weed working on you.

TONY: I know. I know you're right. But people like me need the weed to glimpse what people like you are doing to us. You're right to keep off it, because if you didn't you'd be so far ahead of us we'd never know what was happening and you could take advantage of us.

TANYA: I wouldn't do that.

TONY: Shame. But you did. As a kid. That's what you were doing all the time. Everybody loved you and was jealous of you, boy, girl, adult. You were bewitching. And when you sang in choir, you lifted us all up and transported us. You took advantage of us because you couldn't help yourself. Oh, that's beautiful. That's a revelation. So, you don't remember 'hot?' or 'cold?'.

TANYA: No.

TONY: I'll show you. Sit down here.

He rises to allow her to sit in his seat, which she does with a measure of curiosity. When she is seated he crouches and touches her ankle.

Stick your legs out.

39

TANYA: Why?

He indicates, she does so. He replaces his hands on her ankles.

TONY: Hot?

TANYA: What is this?

TONY: No. You're supposed to say 'yes', or 'no'.

TANYA: I would've remembered this.

TONY: Hot?

TANYA: No. What is the point of this?

TONY: You'll see. (*Moves hand higher.*) Hot?

TANYA: Hang on. No.

TONY: (*Hand higher.*) Hot?

TANYA: No. Hey, I remember this. That's not how you play it.

TONY: Isn't it?

TANYA: No. You're supposed to say, "Are you nervous?"

TONY: What?

TANYA: Look, you sit down and I'll show you.

They exchange places.

Legs out. (*Hands on his ankles.*) Are you nervous?

TONY: That's right! I remember now!

TANYA: And you just keep on going like that.

TONY: Carry on then.

TANYA: No, it's just a kid's game.

TONY: No, go on, see.

TANYA: (*Starting from base.*) Are you nervous?

TONY: Nah.

TANYA: (*Hand higher.*) Are you nervous?

TONY: No.

TANYA: (*Uncertain.*) Are you nervous?

TONY: (*Certain.*) No.

TANYA: (*Close to his crotch.*) Are you nervous?

TONY: (*Seductive.*) Definitely... not.

TANYA: You're doing this on purpose. I'm not going to make your day.

TONY: Who said you would.

TANYA: I can't play this! I can't have played it more than once.

TONY: My turn now.

TANYA: Kill it Tony. (*Cooling the atmosphere.*) We're past all that now.

TONY: Yeah. And we never ever got there. Our folks thought we would.

TANYA: Always getting pushed together.

TONY: I dreamt it would happen one day. You and me. I thought dreams were meant to come true.

TANYA: And nightmares?

TONY: This guy, Nic?

TANYA: What?

TONY: Seems to have built his dreams around you.

TANYA: He can't tell a dream from a nightmare. I'm a nightmare.

41

TONY: Deal straight with me Tanya. I recognise the vibe when it's going down.

TANYA: It's nothing. It's got nothing to do with you anyway.

TONY: You know I know you. Like, I ain't seen you for, how long: five years? But I know you. You ain't changed so much. Lines starting to embed themselves in your features, curves ain't so round, but it's you. I recognise you. Outside and in.

TANYA: So. Tell me. What d'you see?

TONY: I'm gonna be hard on you here now, 'cos I can see a lot of bullshit going on.

TANYA: Me am woman. No man can give me harder than I give meself.

TONY: Yeah, that's what I see. A bitch on heat that's gorged herself so much on the white man's pork that she don't know what next to eat.

TANYA: What?

TONY: You heard. You've bought in so deeply to the white man's world you can't even tell when it's you that's fucking you.

TANYA: Where's this come from?

TONY: From watching you tonight.

TANYA: No. From smoking that spliff. 'Cos I don't think you know what you just said.

TONY: I think I do.

TANYA: If you'd used a rusty razor to hack through our umbilical chord you couldn't have cut the tie with any more hurt.

TONY: Somebody's got to say something to you Tanya. 'Cos you're losing it.

TANYA: I don't want to hear any more! You overstepped the mark there! However well you think you know me, I ain't bitch to you!

TONY: D'you know how long I've waited for you?

TANYA: Nothing we've been through as kids gives you the right to talk to me like that. Nothing.

TONY: All my life. All my life! From when we were small.

TANYA: Fuck you Tony! Fuck you! What the fuck gives you the right to think you can talk to me like that!

TONY: Loving you Tanya! Loving you gives me the right! Like I've always done.

TANYA: To abuse me!

TONY: I'm trying to make you see –

TANYA: You think bullying me is the way to make me see

TONY: I'm not bullying –

TANYA: This is love?

TONY: Sometimes we need –

TANYA: You're wrong! (*Emphatic.*) You are wrong! Do you want to know about Nic?

TONY: I don't care about him.

TANYA: Well I do. I do! He has cared for me, done so many things for me, I'll never be able to repay him.

TONY: Good for him – good for you!

TANYA: Care and consideration, that's what he's shown me. When my personal battles have threatened to separate body from mind from spirit. When I've been on the edge of that black thing called frustration, madness, the black hole – he was there. I've been in another world. Nobody understands. Inside me are confusions, contradictions, and so much frustration it could suck in a galaxy. Nic never understood, he couldn't, but he was there. Support. Love. Kindness. And tenderness. That's what kept me together. You don't know what the madness is. If I sing, it will all come out, that's what I don't want.

TONY: You think I don't know what the madness is? You think I've come down here for polite conversation? You think after living through the malevolence of this united white man's kingdom I don't know the black hole of frustration and inertia. It's hard. What we do. It's not easy. When you want to say – hang on; I've got an idea; I know the solution; let me have a go. (*Drawn inward.*) Let me solve that problem, for you; I can do it... I know, I can. And the eyes look round and they don't see you. You're just a black hole, absorbing all the light, invisible to the naked eye. But you're there. You can feel your weight. You know you're there. Aren't you? So you console yourself, in your room at night, on your own; illuminated by the glow from the monitor. The one thing that confirms existence. Watching the pixels dance their dance of magic. Listening to the dance of the music. Dancing in time to the light on the screen. And the music is beautiful. It makes you cry. It makes you cry, because you're so sad. No-one can hear it. You're invisible. No-one believes in you. At work, at play. You're a black hole... full of captured energy. Your function is to absorb all the shit from the cesspool around you. Take it, like a man...

TANYA: Or a woman...

They look at each other.

TONY: Yeah. Or a woman.

TANYA: (*Holding out arms.*) Come here.

They embrace for a long time. **Track 4** *plays on its metronomic rhythm. Eventually they separate.*

Don't get into the music business. It steals your spirit. Leaves you empty and uncertain.

TONY: Look I'm sorry. I don't normally... go on like that.

TANYA: No. You don't have to –

TONY: Yes. I hate that, 'bitch' and all that aggression. That's no way for people to talk to each other is it?

TANYA: It communicates, I suppose.

TONY: Yeah, but the wrong message. I was disappointed. I was looking forward to...

TANYA: What's this riff.

TONY: Nothing, I just set it up.

TANYA: It's nice

TONY: You're easily pleased.

TANYA: Don't you believe it.

Time passes.

TONY: When I realised what Nic was up to, I started to get excited. The thought that people would actually hear what goes on inside my head, inside my machine. Ah well, close enough for jazz.

TANYA: Nic's a tough cookie. He can do it. The trampling over people. Nobody's going to do that to me again. Ever. I've been through it. But if you can crack it, imagine the things you can do. (*Relaxing.*) I like this track. Tony. I'm sorry. I didn't mean to get you into this mess.

TONY: Sorry, doesn't question the answer. Hold on.

He goes over to the DB-2 re-mixing the sound.

TANYA: What?

TONY: Everything sounds so muddy. I can hardly bear to listen to it.

TANYA: Question the answer?

TONY: Mm. The question to the answer that is 'yes'.

TANYA: I must be passively spliffing, or I'm missing something.

TONY: Don't worry you'll get it. Lock onto my thoughts. (*Pause.*) This might sound like a strange question, after what I said. But, is my music commercial?

TANYA: By no stretch. Was that the question to the answer yes?

TONY: No.

TANYA: Nah. To be commercial you have to convince 'them', the suits. 'Cos, let's face it, what they recognise as music is just so much noise. Otherwise they just stop you in your tracks. I tried to take control of my music, and they told me I was killing my career. Then they went and murdered it to prove they were right. I've had my battles, and lost them all. I won't fight without a strategy. Not anymore.

TONY: Which is?

TANYA: This. (*Holding up spools.*) This was the foundation of my strategy.

TONY: Quite a route to end up in a cul-de-sac.

TANYA: There's one song I want to rework. *Angel Eyes*, my first real go at song writing. The lyrics have gone over and over in my head. Oh God, you should hear it like I hear it in my temple. And when I heard the way you put layers of sound down and moved the ideas around, it was like a revelation. God I'd love to get that one out. (*Stopping.*) What am I gonna do?

TONY: What are the options?

TANYA: I don't know. I only know things when I'm doing them.

TONY: It's not possible not to know in a binary opposition.

TANYA: Huh?

TONY: Shall we all pack up and go home...?

TANYA: Or?

TONY: Shall we stay and produce something special? Remember what the answer was.

TANYA: Is this the question? (*Pause for thought.*) Yes. We could, I suppose just play around – we could work on *Angel Eyes*.

TONY: We should listen to the original.

TANYA: Yeah, why don't we. (*Going to door.*) Where's Nic. I hope he's alright. The front door's open. Nic.

TONY: He'll be with his 'mate' and his vodka in the park, rehearsing for a future where the answer is no.

TANYA: Nic has stood by me.

TONY: Don't have to justify him to me. I don't have to like him.

TANYA: No. But he's our double agent, remember?

TONY: Double agent is just another name for traitor. Remember.

TANYA: Some people imagine black women are half a beat behind. But in strict tempo I think we're half a beat in front.

At this moment, NIC re-enters.

NIC: I've been in the park. That poor git. Worn himself out. Just sitting there in the dark. Wonder how he ended up like that? In void of hope. What can save people like him?

TONY: Isn't that a foolish question, when the answer's Money?

NIC: Yes. Money for God's sake.

TANYA: World doesn't have to revolve round money.

NIC: But it does.

NIC looks at TANYA, who looks at TONY, who looks at NIC.

TANYA: I've changed my mind. I want to work. I want to achieve something tonight. Not for your meeting Nic. For myself.

NIC: Art for art's sake?

TANYA: That's not the way I see it.

NIC: However you see it. (*Hugging her.*) Thank you Tanya. (*Without releasing her.*) You're saving me from the black hole. (*Kiss.*)

TONY watches this, and moves over to his computer.

NIC releases TANYA and begins to organise the mixer area. He fast forwards the Teac, looking for a particular track.

Track 5

Angel Eyes

NIC: Time to celebrate!

NIC pulls out a small twist of silver foil. TANYA prepares herself to sing. Everybody's rhythm changes as the tempo increases.

TANYA: (*Resigned.*) Nic.

NIC: If you'd like to venture into the dark heart Tanya, we can sound-check the mike.

TANYA: Sound-check, check-sound-check, check-sound-check, check-round-check, check-down-check, check-in-check, check-out-check, check-doubt-check, check-fire-check, check-rain-check, check-pleasure-check, check-pain-check, check-future-check, checked-past-check...

Exhausting her invention, TANYA enters the sound booth.

NIC: (*To TONY.*) You'll need these.

TONY: What's that?

NIC: Samples.

TONY: I've got a whole library of samples.

NIC: No, use these. I had a mate take samples from the masters – the original instrumentation – so you can feather in sounds where we need them. A little patching up.

TONY: Hang on, I'm confused. What am I supposed to do with them?

NIC: We've laid down the tracks, but there are a few holes where I'd like to tighten things up a bit, add a bit of dynamic and stuff. You put these in the machine, I'll let you know how I want it to come out.

TONY: Well, what format are they in, for a start?

NIC: Dunno. Dunno what you mean.

TONY: There's no way I can use them if they aren't in the right format.

NIC: You might be out of a job then.

TONY: You can't just shove a bunch of discs into a computer and expect them to work.

NIC: Not my department. You sort it out. Look, when I called you you told me a whole lot of technical stuff about your system, right?

TONY: Yeah.

NIC: I passed that on to my mate, and he did whatever was needed to get what I needed onto those bits of plastic. He assured me they would work.

TANYA: (*Emerging from booth.*) Is there a problem?

NIC: Nothing our genius here can't handle. There you are. (*Hands over discs.*)

TANYA: Tony?

TONY: This is crazy.

TANYA: Is it going to work Tony.

TONY: We'll see.

NIC: Are you going to check your mike Tanya?

TONY reluctantly busies himself with loading-up the discs. NIC engrosses himself preparing lines of cocaine between working on the mikes.

TANYA: Is there no more light in here?

NIC: I'm afraid that's it my baby. Treat it like mood lighting.

TANYA: Bad mood lighting.

TANYA picks one of two microphones on stands.

(*At booth door.*) Somebody's been eating this thing!

NIC: (*As she re-enters.*) Is it on?

TANYA: Sorry Nic?

NIC: Is it on – the mike?

TANYA: (*At booth door.*) I can't hear a word you're saying. Isn't there any talk-back.

NIC: There should be. Give me a minute.

TANYA: Is this the place you used to go on about?

NIC: What? Oh yeah.

TANYA: And you actually did it in there?

NIC: Yes, but we don't need to...

TANYA: That why it smells of fish?

NIC: Tanya...

TANYA: They feed fish waste to battery chickens you know?

NIC: Uh-huh.

TANYA: I've given up eating chicken. And I only buy free range eggs. Imagine having to fill all these egg boxes. Like a machine.

NIC: (*Absently.*) Yes, must be terrible.

TANYA: Wonder what they think about while they're sitting there plopping their eggs, eating their fish guts?

NIC: Could you pass me a couple of phono leads Tony?

TONY: Sure.

NIC: And get me a stereo-phono to canon.

TONY: They're loading. Doesn't mean they'll play.

TANYA: Do you know why they use egg boxes?

NIC: Mm?

TANYA: On the walls?

TONY: Causes interference. Kills reverb. (*To NIC.*) There you go.

NIC: Thanks.

TANYA: Because its cheap – get it!

NIC: It also cuts down the noise from the hens' crowing.

TANYA: Cocks crow. Hens cluck.

NIC: Will you get in there and try out that mike.

TANYA: Why don't the cock's have to go into those stinking coops.

NIC: (*As she enters.*) Sing, warm yourself up. I'll find your mike.

With that she re-enters the booth, where she picks up the mike and begins to sing **Track 5 – Angel Eyes**.

Ah! Can you hear me Tanya?

She gives a thumbs up, while continuing to sing.

NIC: Good! Mission control we have contact!

TONY: I'm amazed this stuff is loading.

NIC: Counting down to take off! Now I just have to find Tanya.

TONY: I reckon she'll be on fifteen or sixteen.

NIC: Let's have a go... no.

TONY: Try toggling between A and B.

NIC follows these instructions. TANYA's voice comes through, but it is broken up.

NIC: Loose wire.

TONY: Bad mike lead I'd say.

NIC: Possibly. Tanya, try the other mike. You not set up yet?

TONY: Taking a while to load.

As NIC brings up the fader we hear TANYA on the speakers.

NIC: (*On talk-back.*) Sweet babes, just sweet.

TONY: There, we're loaded. Anything from the tape?

NIC: No. You have a go. I need to charge my batteries.

TONY: Uh? Oh. Yeah.

They exchange places. NIC taking his 'tramlines'.

NIC: So, what do you think of this Internet?

TONY: It has its uses.

NIC: But is it a good thing? I'm curious.

TONY: When I was born, somebody'd already invented the wheel. I don't ask whether the wheel is a good thing. A wheel on a tank is bad, a wheel on an ambulance is good.

NIC: Simple as that?

TONY: Simple as that.

NIC: Shouldn't we think of the morals of things we create?

TONY: Think about them, yeah. Then get on with it. The only people who ask pointless questions about whether the Internet is a good or bad thing, are the people who want to control it – or the ones who think the world was a better place in the past.

TANYA: (*Emerging.*) What's the hold up?

TONY: I reckon with that we should get...

He adjusts a few settings on the mixer and presses play on the Teac. As he slides the fader we begin to hear TANYA singing one of the tape-tracks. TONY makes a few adjustments, the sound quality improves.

TANYA: Nic, find *Angel Eyes*, I want Tony to hear it.

NIC: Sure.

NIC takes over and scans through the tape, stopping and playing occasionally, as he searches through the tracks. Flashes of sound are heard, corresponding to the different tracks. (Tape-Tracks 1 to 4.)

Eventually tape-track 5 is reached which plays as **Track 5**, *while NIC resumes his 'white lining'.*

TANYA: (*To TONY.*) This is *Angel Eyes*, the song I was telling you about.

NIC: Tanya. I've laid down a line for you.

TANYA: No thanks Nic.

NIC: It's Rolls Royce.

TANYA: I've told you, no thanks.

NIC: Tony?

TONY: It's too white for me.

NIC: OK. You stick to the bush.

TANYA and TONY watch NIC snort, as tape-track 5 plays through.

Phew!

TONY: It's... it's OK.

TANYA: And I've got new lyrics!

TONY: Mm.

TANYA: Sounds different to how I remembered though. Is this the last take we did Nic?

TONY: This system won't do it justice.

NIC: We only did one take.

TANYA: (*To NIC.*) Are these the masters?

NIC: Yes.

TANYA: (*Mixing.*) Sounds terrible.

NIC: Well you were a little out of it last time we were in the studio.

TANYA: I remembered this being good.

NIC: We should listen to *Once Is Enough*. That's definitely got potential. I'll wind on –

TANYA: No Nic. I want to hear the rest of this.

NIC: What's the point. *Once Is Enough* is the only one came close to being any good.

TANYA: What d'you mean?

NIC: Well the others were nice ideas, but they were never gonna come off. *Once Is Enough* is the only one that amounts to consequence.

TANYA: How can you say that?

NIC: It was going to be your next single.

TANYA: Only because it's the most commercial. It's a ditty, nothing more.

NIC: Rearrange it, make it modern, it's perfect.

TANYA: Perfect for what? It's a pop song. It's inconsequential.

NIC: You heard it two years ago. Listen to it now. Then talk about it.

NIC stops the tape and begins to wind forward so that what we hear is 'monkey chatter'.

TANYA: Nic! I was listening to that!

NIC: You just said yourself that *Angel Eyes* is rubbish! Now listen to *Once Is Enough*. I'm telling you it's a hit. You're not a song writer Tanya, it's your voice that we're after.

TANYA: I can't believe I'm hearing this. My song is crap?

NIC: Don't over-react! If we want to go for a song that will re-launch you, *Once Is Enough* is the one to go for. Believe me.

TANYA looks at him in amazement.

TANYA: (*Quietly.*) Even you.

With that she moves directly to the sound booth, closing the door and turning out the interior lights. It is a moment before NIC absorbs what has happened.

NIC: Tanya! Tanya. Don't be childish.

He opens the door, she pulls it shut.

This is pathetic. Don't be stupid. Come out.

TONY crosses to his computer, where he sits and begins to play **Track 6**, *which is a collection of samples from the master tape. The end of the tape is reached and the spool spins on.*

Track 6

Showdown

As **Track 6** *plays. NIC is drawn to the Teac, where he threads the end of the tape back onto the spool and begins to rewind. TONY draws out another spliff, which he lights up, as he concentrates on his activities.*

NIC: Nothing to say?

TONY: What's the point. You won't hear anyway.

NIC: Listen, I'll play it for you.

TONY: Play it for yourself.

NIC: Tanya and I agreed it was going to be her first single.

He finds the beginning of tape-track 12 and starts it playing.

Listen to this.

TONY: You just don't get it do you! You really are incapable of interpreting what's going on here aren't you!

NIC: (*Cool.*) And what exactly is that? If you have insight into the inner workings of everybody's mind, share it.

TONY: If I thought any attempt to talk to you would be worth the waste of breath, I would.

NIC: Too difficult to explain? Beyond my comprehension? A black thing is it?

TONY: Damn right it is! You can't goad me. Don't pursue me unless you're going to follow me all the way. The truth as I see it.

NIC: Oh no, don't spare me. I've grown very quickly bored with watching you sit back, say nothing, and still criticise. Give me the truth, I'm fascinated.

TONY: You're going to have to learn something here. You know.

NIC: (*Challenge.*) Teach me.

TONY: You'd love it if I communicated to you with violence.

NIC: If it comes natural to you...

TONY: No. I'm going to tell you something. The secret you want to know, about the black thing. And I can guarantee, that by the end, you won't have understood a word of it. OK?

NIC: Sounds fine.

TONY: (*Offering spliff.*) Here, take a toke.

NIC: Thanks no. (*Holding up silver foil.*) I have my own brand.

TONY: There. You're off. You think I'm just offering you drugs.

NIC: Well it's not a liquorice stick is it? I don't want that stuff. It puts me to sleep. I need my energy up.

TONY: There. The first secret. Take it. It lowers your energy to the point that you're almost asleep, that's the first lesson. Understanding where I'm coming from is about understanding my energy. Do you know anything about chemistry? (*Passes spliff.*)

NIC: What? A fucking chemistry lesson now. (*Takes toke.*)

TONY: Go with me. No, smoke it. I've learned what I know of chemistry from late night Open University. You ever hear of Water and Stone – different ways of thinking?

NIC: No.

TONY: You're thinking like a rock. Think fluid, and go with me.

NIC: If experience has taught me anything, it's to be suspicious, sceptical if you like. I'm not throwing that away on your say so.

TONY: In other words simple answers to questions when you don't even know what the question is.

NIC: I know what the question is alright.

TONY: Keep it moving. (*Collects spliff.*) Well?

NIC: You. You don't engage do you. That's a black thing isn't it? To stand outside of everything. Like you've got a secret. Like you're superior.

TONY: (*Broad smile.*) There is a simple answer there, but we're not after simple answers are we? Tanya engaged with you didn't she?

NIC: Meaning? Ah, that's different. That's very different. That's a man and a woman. That's love. No. It's you. You, you black boys! It's you men I'm talking about. Tanya's different, treats people like people. She hasn't got a chip on her shoulder. It's the one's with the chips on their shoulders I'm talking about. Like you. (*Shakes head.*) Joint's gone straight to my head.

The light goes on in the booth. We see TANYA.

TONY: This is getting interesting now. Chemistry then.

NIC: Where does that come in?

TONY: Between a man and a woman, the way you tell it. But it comes in here as well. (*Holds up spliff.*) In this. All the drugs we consume. You've been drugging yourself up to the gills all night.

NIC: And you've been abstemious I suppose.

TONY: This isn't about comparison. I use a different cocktail. We all do. That's what really rubs up the belly of this united white man's kingdom.

NIC: Drugs?

TONY: Who controls them.

NIC: You think that's what it comes down to? That's simple.

TONY: No, not so simple. Onto the why. Why they will have to accept this, one day. (*Holds up spliff.*) You see, I wasn't brought up on this stuff. Here. (*Passes joint.*) My parents would dispossess me. But they don't understand the social, the economic purpose of it. That's another subject I learned on the Open University. They should ban it. Information is power. That's the thing about the internet. The reason they'll legalise this, is because they'll have got control of it. It is simple isn't it? They'll have wrested control of it from the hands and the minds of those to whom it is indigenous. They will have worked out what it does. With their chemistry sets. Like tea from China – India. Coffee from Brazil. Diamonds and Uranium in South Africa. King sugar in the Caribbean. All drugs in their own way.

NIC: Uranium? A drug? (*Returns spliff.*)

TONY: What is a drug? Something to make you feel better? The Nuclear deterrent?

TANYA emerges from the booth, unnoticed by them.

NIC: There're none so uneducated as the self-educated. Too much Learning Zone has confused you. You talk about things and you don't question whether they have good effects or bad effects. You're immoral.

TONY: Capitalism was also invented before I was born. Is that about morality? No. It's about commodities. Things to be owned, controlled, enslaved. Sometimes I think I only smoke spliff as a form of protest. But it's more important than that. It keeps my mind operating differently from yours. I'd hate to think the way you do. To see the world with your mind-set; your thought patterning – mind set in stone.

NIC: You're talking like our brains are programmable computers. They're not, we're human beings.

TONY: Water and stone? See, you look at that machine and ask what's good or bad about it. It's an inanimate object. We have the ability to accept thoughts, feelings, ideas.

NIC: This is bollocks! I asked you a direct question and you've just gone off on a big tangent. Why don't you engage with what I'm talking about, black people with chips on their shoulders.

TONY: Engage? On your level? No. Because I'm not just the colour of my skin. And because I want you to engage on mine. (*Offers joint.*)

NIC: No, I can't take any more of that stuff. My head's jumbled. Is it because you're frightened that we're gonna steal all your women?

TONY: (*Continuous laughter.*)

NIC: No. It's a serious question.

TONY: (*Still laughing.*) I shouldn't laugh, it's not funny.

NIC: Well?

TONY: If it were that, don't you think it's more likely the other way round –

TANYA: (*Seething.*) I don't know what game you two are playing. But I've never witnessed a more worthless conversation. It's the same thing. Always the same thing. Property. Women as your property. So you can bargain with us and exchange us. We're not your slaves. Shut that noise off!

The music stops.

If neither of you have any respect for women, I don't want to hear about it – not on my time. I don't care if you want to get out of your heads and divide the world between you. Because from where I'm standing neither of you have got much to offer anybody. All you have are your relationships with the sound of your own voices, your drugs, and these toys. Well, I'm not a boy toy, I'm a working woman and I want to do some work. Nic. I need to speak to you – in the chicken coop. Now!

She goes into the booth, leaving the door ajar. NIC follows her in, closing the door behind him. TONY watches them go.

Track 7

All Is Confusion

Moving over to the mixer, TONY rewinds the tape on the Teac. He is searching for tape-track 5 – Angel Eyes. As he stands at the mixer, something occurs to him. Turning his back on the booth, he leans against the mixer and eases the mike fader up. We are able to hear what is being said in the booth. TONY returns his computer. When he has found the track he is searching for he plays it. He samples and edits their conversation.

NIC: Come on. You need something to unwind you. You're as tight as a spring.

TANYA: And you think white powders will do it? This isn't fiction Nic. What would loosen me up, is having my opinions take seriously, not pushed aside like so much annoyance.

NIC: I'm sorry. I know I should've... I didn't... I'm sorry.

TANYA: Sorry don't make it happen Nic. I told you. I'm not a child.

NIC: You were never a child. Not to me. Never that. C'mon It'll give you an edge, make you feel clearer.

TANYA: I'm as clear as day follows night.

*TONY is composing **Track 7**. Sampling a cross fade begins. As the lights in the booth come up, the lights in the studio go down. We* *see TANYA and NIC, with TONY in silhouette as he moves between mixer and computer, snatching and mixing their conversation.*

NIC: And you don't fancy any of Tony's giggle-sticks.

TANYA: You're not taking on board anything I'm telling you. I don't need any drugs. I'm off it. All. For good. I'm not going to screw myself up on that stuff like you have.

NIC: Hang on Tanya, it's not this, it's... it's...

TANYA: See, you can't even talk straight.

NIC: I'm-I'm-I'm fine, I'm OK.

TANYA: No you're not. My mind's in better shape, my body feels like my own. And I'm not wasting any more of my money on drugs. I'm never going back to that place you took me.

NIC: Don't give me that Tanya. You weren't a child. You knew exactly what you were getting into. It was hard to restrain you. I didn't take you anywhere. Except to success. What you did with it was your responsibility. (*Sniff.*) I've got to clear my head. That smoke has fucked with my mind!

TANYA: Look at you Nic. You're falling apart. Kick it. It's screwing you up.

NIC: Screwing me up? This is my creative tool.

TANYA: It's not a tool. It's a place to hide.

NIC: From?

TANYA: Fear of failure. I know that. I know what's going on. I know you Nic. I'm not speeding into that trap. I've learned to deal with my fear. You could as well.

NIC: You sound like you found God.

TANYA: What makes you think I ever lost him, or her for that matter. God is a spirit not a person.

NIC: Oh God save us from God's sex change. If the omniscient one has become an hermaphrodite, no wonder you're confused. This purified world you want to get hold of is already too contaminated to separate out. Why bother?

TANYA: Because how I live my life matters. It's not confusion. I know it's all mixed up. All the ideas are getting mixed up. I don't want to separate them or purify them. What I want is spiritual honesty. How can you be honest when your mind's swimming in cocaine?

NIC: Why is it that converts are so certain they're right.

TANYA: It's not a question of right or wrong, good or bad. It's about self preservation. Look at yourself. You're running scared. Since I got out of the business, my life has improved – the quality of my life, the things that are important – my health. I've learned to live properly. To live a good life.

NIC: Spare me Tanya. I'm sorry. The moment I hear anyone talking like that all I see is charity singles and free publicity. Save the whale, save the rain forest, save everyone in the entire world. Give the punters that line, but we know what it's really about. Look at Tony. Filling himself with altruism and political truth. He's tiny. He sits in an office doling out pennies to the unemployed to save himself from being one of them. He's frightened of taking the risk of committing himself to what he really wants to do. Offer him a record deal and he'd bite your hand off. We all have our price.

TANYA: Maybe we do Nic. But no one's offered me mine yet. And Tony ain't gonna be bought cheap.

NIC: Huh. So, did you and he ever...?

TANYA: Oh, men! That's got nothing to do with you Nic, or why we're here. And I want you to understand that. I like you, but I'm no longer your concubine whose opinions you can ignore. It's business between us from now on.

NIC: Unfinished business for me.

TANYA: End of story Nic. Sorry.

NIC: That's OK. If you don't want this, I'll have it.

He snorts another couple of lines.

You've become hard Tanya

TANYA: Thanks for the lessons.

NIC: You've become a witch.

TANYA: I always was, you just never noticed.

NIC: I don't understand you anymore Tanya.

TANYA: You've become more cynical. We used to be able to talk.

NIC: Let's talk about *Once Is Enough*.

TANYA: I feel things about *Angel Eyes*. I may be wrong, but I feel it. That's what I want us to work on. That's all I want us to work on.

NIC: Angel Eyes. *Angel Eyes* it is then... my baby. Before my head explodes. Tony will be getting curious about us.

TONY: (*Stopping the machines.*) Wrong.

A cross-fade begins, the reverse of the previous.

TANYA: I hope we connected Nic. We need to, or we can't help each other.

NIC: I've always helped you in the past, don't intend to stop now.

TANYA: Thanks. You're a friend. (*A kiss.*)

TONY brings the faders down on their conversation. All sound has stopped. NIC and TANYA emerge from the sound booth.

NIC: Right. Play what you got.

TONY: What?

NIC: (*Upbeat.*) *Angel Eyes*. We've decided that's the one we're working on. Let's hear what's on the computer.

TONY: Right. Problem.

TANYA: What?

TONY: I've got nothing on my screen called *Angel Eyes*.

NIC takes a large slug of vodka and slumps into the sofa.

NIC: Great!

Track 8

The Chicken & The Egg (Inc. Programme Change)

TANYA's eyes meet TONY's.

TANYA: It isn't on there?

TONY: I didn't say that. I said there's nothing on here called *Angel Eyes*. What there are though, are files numbered one to twelve. Presumably, it's one of those. Where did it come in sequence?

NIC: Five

TANYA: Yeah. It would've come at the end of side one on an LP. That's where most of my favourite tracks came when I was a kid. Funny how you remember these things.

TONY: I'll play track five then.

TONY sets the computer going. A strange melange of sounds is heard.

NIC: What's that?

TONY: Track five. Not sure what's happening.

He re-starts it. With the same result.

NIC: I'll tell you what's happening. The poor beast is totally confused.

TANYA: What?

TONY: Hang on. This isn't in General Midi is it?

NIC: What the hell is that?

He makes some adjustments. Some of the sounds drop out.

TONY: I don't know why it's doing this.

TANYA: What's it doing?

TONY: Can't you hear? I'll isolate one track.

He does so. What is heard is the same rhythmic sequence, shifting between different instrumental voices.

NIC: That's supposed to be the drum pattern. What's happening?

TONY: It's... it's switching voices. Everything else is playing the drum pattern, except the drum. That's strange?

NIC: I thought you were tuned in to this thing.

TONY: First time this has ever happened. Let me think.

TANYA: What is it Tony?

TONY: I don't know. Each track on here is supposed to drive a specific voice, but for some reason, the tracks are being assigned to different voices. They keep switching.

Leaving it running he rises from the screen and moves around the space. Pondering, having let it run, a pattern emerges.

Hear that!

TANYA: What? Yeah. That's the wrong orchestration.

NIC: What's happening?

TONY: I'll stop it.

He does so.

NIC: Could you explain what's going on – in simple terms – because that isn't right.

TONY: Simple answers for complex ideas eh?

NIC: If you understand the thing, translate for it.

TONY: Yes... and no.

NIC: Meaning?

TONY: Yes I sort of understand it. But no, I can't translate. It's got a language of it's own.

NIC: Now we can't even understand the bloody things.(*Patiently.*) Can you tell me, in technical, or any terms you like, what has just happened here.

TONY: Maybe. As long as you understand that the computer has a logic of it's own. It is absolute about it's logic.

TANYA: I'm sorry Tony, I might be stupid, but I don't know what you're talking about.

TONY: I'm trying to find a way to explain it. See that booth there – the window. Imagine the window is the computer screen; it's window on the world. There's no door, just that window into computer world – the booth. You with me?

TANYA: Yeah.

NIC: I just want an answer.

TONY: Water and stone remember. So. Load up your brain with imagination. Gigabytes of it.

TANYA: Gigabytes?

TONY: A lot. A hell of a lot of imagination. I know, I'll go in there.

TONY puts up the mike fader on the mixer and enters the sound booth, picking up the microphone. The lights begin their cross fade; up inside the booth, down in the studio. But this time the light inside the booth is blue. TONY is heard on the speakers.

I'm something inside the computer called the Central Processing Unit – CPU. I'm like a controller because I can connect up lots of different things in computer world, the computer's brain, but I'm guided by strict logic, binary oppositions. There's lots of information in here. There're lots of chickens, laying eggs. Each egg is a piece of information, like a note. And I'm the cock.

NIC: I don't believe this.

TANYA: Shush.

TONY: Each egg sits in a particular cup in the egg boxes. When I pick up an egg in here and throw it into the air, it plays a note on a piano. I'm juggling I'm playing a trill, I'm holding them in Random Access Memory – RAM. Tanya could you go to my computer and move the arrow on the screen till its over a file with the name "T's Tune". It's about there on the screen.

He indicates this position by pointing on the inside of the sound booth window. TANYA crosses to the computer, but stands frozen in front of it.

TANYA: I can't. I don't understand these things.

TONY: Tanya. I'm inside the computer and I'm telling you what to do.

NIC crosses to join her.

The mouse. Move the mouse along the table.

NIC: (*To TANYA.*) The mouse is that thing.

TANYA: I know what a mouse is!

TONY: The arrow is presently here. It needs to move to about here. Don't be afraid. I'll let you know if you do it wrong.

NIC: We've got the mouse. The arrow is moving.

TANYA: He can't hear you.

TONY: When it's over the file named *T's Tune*, click the mouse. It's like squeezing it's neck.

TANYA: Hey yeah!

NIC: We've done it! It's changing.

TONY: You aren't there yet. Concentrate. There's a button marked *Play*, here on the screen. (*Indicates.*) I'm juggling in RAM remember

TANYA: I see it.

NIC: We've got to move the mouse onto it.

TANYA: I know, I know.

TONY: Move the arrow onto the button, as before.

NIC: You've gone past it.

TANYA: Leave me!

TONY: When you're there, click the mouse.

NIC: Squeeze it's neck!

TONY: If you've done it right, it'll start running. You'll hear music.

Music begins to play **Track 8**. *A slow bass sequence. TANYA and NIC celebrate. TANYA giving TONY the thumbs up.*

NIC: Teamwork!

TANYA: We've done it!

NIC: This is a piece of piss.

TONY: I'm RAM and I'm juggling these notes; these eggs.

TONY mimes juggling.

(*Continuing to juggle.*) There's something in this room I haven't told you about.

NIC: Hey, you can't do that!

TANYA: Button it Nic, I'm on a wavelength here.

TONY: On the floor and the ceiling and the other three walls, there are windows, exactly like the one you're looking through, but they've got no glass in them. Open windows right.

NIC: What're you standing on then?

TANYA: Nic!

TONY: And on the other side of those windows are rooms full of other hens laying eggs. Also in those rooms are windows on the ceilings, floors and walls

TANYA: Hang on. Let me get this straight. I'm losing it.

NIC: I'm stoned aren't I?

TONY: I'm in all these rooms juggling eggs in RAM, I'm free to move into any of them I choose, be in all of them at the same time. I'm going to exit this room and enter another. And I will carry on juggling these eggs as I pass through the window.

TANYA: Oh no! (*Hand on mouth.*)

TONY: I'm going... (*Moving out of view.*) Now!

As he does so the lights cross fade from blue to red. On his signal, the music keeps tempo but changes instrumentation to a piano.

TANYA: He did it! He did it!

TONY: That's the easy part over. I'm going to pick up an egg, a note, from this room. And move to another.

As he carries out these instructions the music and lights follow.

To complete my opus. I must move from room to room; faster than you can blink; juggling more and more eggs. Listen.

Now a coherent musical piece emerges, multi-instrumental. As the lights chase the music, TONY's actions become more frenetic.

Now if I pick up an egg from the blue room, and put it back down in the red room, or vice versa, then things start going wrong. That's what's happening to *Angel Eyes*.

Into the mix appear snatches of NIC and TANYA's conversation from earlier. They begin to respond to this fact. Both moving away from the computer.

TANYA: What?

NIC: Where's this come from?

TANYA: Tony! (*Cold anger.*) Tony!

TONY registers that the illusion is broken, emerging from the booth door. Quickly he moves to the computer. He stops the machine. Music and lights cut suddenly. Reality returns.

Tony. How the hell did we get in there?

TONY: I don't know. I don't know what happened.

TANYA: You were listening!

TONY: No, I, well I sampled bits that's all. But it must've... look, that shouldn't have happened.

TANYA: I don't like this. I don't like this at all.

NIC: There's something obscene going on.

TANYA: That was a private conversation. Understand? Private. Is that what you use this thing for? To snoop on people? It isn't right! It isn't right Tony!

TONY: Oh come on! It's not as if you were talking state secrets! It was an experiment! I've never done it before.

TANYA: You've never had a chance before!

NIC: I needn't worry about morality need I not?

TONY: I don't know why you're fussing. It hasn't harmed anyone.

TANYA: It's harmed me. I didn't come here to be manipulated like this.

TONY: I didn't mean that to happen. I don't know why it did, I'm sorry.

There is inertia. Then TONY sits at his computer, examining the screen.

TANYA: Give me a drink.

NIC: Are you sure you need one?

TANYA: Yes I am! I am sure! Don't treat me like a child!

TANYA throws herself into the sofa where she sits glaring, tension gripping her body. NIC pours some vodka into the glass, holding it out for her. She takes a big swig. NIC goes to sit at the mixer.

Track 9

Black Hole

NIC looks between the two of them.

NIC: I don't know about anyone else, but I don't think things are going very well.

TONY: (*Sullen, for TANYA.*) It wasn't my idea to be here tonight. I've been manipulated as well!

NIC: You are here. And it would be good if you could put that machine of yours to some positive use. Now we know about the chickens and the eggs. The one thing we haven't had, from the machine, is what we want. Can you deliver?

TONY: I've been trying to figure out what went wrong just now. It was playing one file; fine. Then it jumped to another. And now I can't find either. A new one's appeared, "unnamed". The computer has merged two different files into one.

NIC: Meaning?

TONY: Meaning... what? The system's... been corrupted. Shit!

Something has just dawned on him.

The guy who put this stuff on disc for you... he didn't say anything about a virus did he?

NIC: I wouldn't know if he did. Why?

TONY: That's what it must be. A virus has got onto my hard drive.

NIC: Sounds rather unpleasant.

TONY: It's the end. Shit! (*Panicked.*) I'd better switch off. (*Thinking.*) No. God knows what'll happen. Shit! Shit! Shit! That must be it. A virus.

NIC: What does a virus actually do?

TONY: Anything and everything. They create the end of the world, as far as I'm concerned. They're like black holes that suck in information.

NIC: Will we be able to do anything?

TONY: I don't have any protection for this. Can you get hold of this mate of yours?

NIC: I've only got his number at the studio. What time is it?

TONY: Nearly four o'clock.

NIC: He won't be there now. Is this serious?

TONY: Damn! Damn! It could be. I don't know. I don't know what to do. I don't know what the virus might do. I haven't even got any discs, to save some of this stuff. I didn't think. I'll try running another file.

NIC: Try *Angel Eyes*, that's the one we want.

TONY sets **Track 9** *running, It is a version of tape-track 5, Angel Eyes. It plays while TANYA has been observing the crisis. Briefly.*

Sounds fine. Let's go for it quickly, before anything else goes wrong. We've got to get something out tonight. What do you think Tanya?

TANYA: (*Unenthusiastic.*) Yeah. Might as well.

NIC: Into the booth and just sing along, while I balance your mike.

TANYA is not in the mood, but resignedly makes her way to the booth.

Back to the beginning Tony. I'll set your levels at the same time.

TONY: You can't do it from there. I've by-passed that mixer. All my controls are inside the machine.

NIC: You'll have to set levels then. I'll run to record, set to pause. Let's get something down on tape while everything's stable. Where did I put my gear? (*Looks around.*) Forget it. Sound check! Go Tony.

TONY starts the computer. **Track 9** *plays. TANYA begins to sing along with it. We hear her voice being treated and the orchestration being altered as NIC and TONY adjust various settings. Eventually they are happy with the mix.*

OK. Cut it Tony. That's good. It's not perfect, but we'll go at that. Next one's going on tape.

(*On talk-back.*) Great Tanya, you're sounding great. Just needs a bit more life. You sound like somebody died. Go for it this time babes.

A thumbs up from TANYA.

Right. Everybody charge up! (*Nervous.*) Christ I could do with a line. (*To both.*) Let's make it happen! Rolling tape.

He starts the reel-to-reel.

(*In the manner of a toast.*) To wherever the vagaries of technology lead us! Go Tony.

At a high volume the call comes – "Call the police!..." All three are startled.

TANYA: (*From booth.*) What the hell was that?

NIC: Shit!

TONY: Oh no.

The music becomes sporadic and playful then stops. TANYA emerges from the booth. They look at each other. NIC and TANYA look to TONY.

Don't look at me. It's the machine. It's gone crazy!

TANYA enters the sound booth.

Track 10

Mutant

There is a time slip.

TONY: This is unnatural.

NIC: Is it not technology?

TONY: Maybe the mike picked it up.

NIC: Maybe there's a ghost in your machine.

TONY: Wasn't it powerful though! Made me jump out of my skin. Really dynamic.

NIC: But useless. I should be mixing down now You don't know anyone else with a computer – a reliable machine.

TONY: This was reliable until tonight. Besides, the virus is on the discs. Start loading those into other machines and you'll have an epidemic on your hands.

NIC: And you can't de-bug this bugger?

TONY: Out of my range. This machine was a virgin until tonight.

NIC: Look Tony, we're not going to be able to rely on this to get us through are we?

TONY: Not in a linear form. If there's a virus in here, then the software's mutating.

As TANYA speaks from the sound booth, the computer begins to play. A quiet Re-orchestrated version of track 5, this is **Track 10**.

TANYA: You know what I'm beginning to think? I'm beginning to think that this virus isn't in the machine. I think it's in us. What are we trying to do here? Because, I know I got us together for all this, and I'm sorry it's turned out like it has, but I think the problem is me. (*Pause for thought.*) I've never felt like a creative person. I've never known what being creative was. I can sing, but I've always been able to do that. I've never tried to start with nothing and end with something in the end. It's a difficult thing you know, when all the time you're following. Following somebody else's lead. A man, because you're a woman and that's just the way things go. White people, because they're experienced and used to being in control. Parents – because they're your parents. Always being led. Always following. I wanted to try being the one in front. Even when I was fronting my so-called band, Black Orchid, everyone knew what was going on. Even that name comes from the title of a song. There's nothing original about me. I just followed. I want to be the driving force. The creator of something original. I suppose – and this is crazy – I want to feel what God felt, what nature feels. To start with nothing, and create... something.

TANYA leaves the booth.

We've got to grab this moment. Make something out of this chaos. Evolve. I'm lost, but follow me. I trust my feelings and instincts. Yeah, I'm a modern day mutant.

TONY: (*Studying screen.*) This is mad! It's segueing files together.

NIC: Tanya. This is too weird. This isn't what I'm used to. I don't know what to do.

TANYA: I do. Trust me. Just this once.

TANYA hesitates. But NIC has got through to her. "Call the police", jumps out.

Track 11

Untitled

TANYA sits on sofa.

NIC: How can we do anything if it keeps jumping around like that?

TONY: I think Tanya's saying, we should just improvise. I mean, I can control the faders. If I'm sharp, I can mix in real time.

TANYA: I'll just fill, go for repeats, snatch words. Improvise. I know I can do that.

TONY: It's kept the same time code, so you can rely on the rhythm for scansion.

NIC: It'll sound like crap. It will be crap.

TANYA: Who cares! That's the deal.

TONY: It'll be creative. Not crap, more like rap.

NIC: Tanya can't rap, she's never rapped.

TANYA: But I can scat. It's a journey into the unknown. Do you think God knew how it would turn out?

TONY: Curiosity, discovery, invention? What have we got to lose.

NIC: The Demo. I'll make a fool of myself.

TANYA: You've never been at the sharp end of the big new sounds. This could be it.

TONY: It's up to you. Don't do it if the vibe isn't right.

TANYA: Of course. Don't push yourself. If it's too difficult for you.

NIC: Let me think I've got to have a line.

TANYA: No! Everybody does it clean – no more drugs. I couldn't trust you if you were out of your heads.

TONY: Safe. Your rules.

NIC: My blood's pure adrenaline

TANYA: And we just keep going, no matter what happens

TONY: No-one in control! (*Referring to computer.*) This thing has a mind of its own.

TANYA: Once on that roller coaster we don't stop!

NIC: Yeah, how will we know when to stop?

TONY: We're jamming. We'll know. (*Taps screen.*)

TANYA: All I want to do is sing.

NIC: Let's do it then.

TANYA: Are you sure?

NIC: (*Dry.*) Don't I look sure?

He slumps.

Track 12

Once Is Enough
(Angel Eyes Rap/Scratch mix)

There is a look between NIC and TONY.

TANYA: Start the track Tony. We'll have to do this some way.

NIC: Hang on, I'm not ready yet!

TANYA: Doesn't matter. I'm just getting things going.

NIC puts the reel-to-reel in record mode, setting it going.

NIC: OK. Let's go for a long intro. I'm rolling tape, I think. Start the track.

TONY does so. The music that comes out is an uncluttered version of Angel Eyes. TANYA does not move for a while. When she does it is to look at the monitor.

TANYA: Is that the mixer?

TONY: Yeah.

TANYA: Which are the tracks?

TONY: Each one of these.

She collects her bag. Rooting through it, she eventually draws out a lipstick. She approaches the booth, and on the outside of the window she draws a proportional representation of the monitor screen. When she has completed this...

TANYA: Right. (*To TONY.*) If I point to something on my screen, it means I want you to do it on yours.

TONY: Yeah, you bet.

TANYA: (*To NIC.*) I need to know what I'm working with.

NIC: I don't know what the hell is going on.

TANYA: I'm ready now.

She goes into the booth, closing the door. Immediately there is development in the music. NIC looks to TONY, who gives him a shrug. Inside the booth TANYA is still.

TONY: How d'you think she'll do.

NIC: She's a performer. She'll perform. In your own time babes. The audience is waiting.

A new melange comes from the speakers. It is **Track 12**. *As it plays TANYA begins to sing the lyrics to Angel Eyes. Dropping them into this final soundscape where they fit, initially as speech – becoming song. In addition to this the sound booth becomes a concert platform, lights animated in the nature of pop lighting. The studio light* *slowly dims, till TONY and NIC are no more than silhouettes, moving to the complex and constantly changing sounds and rhythms of the music. Track 12 contains scatterings of dialogue and music, from the text of the play. It has a dynamic/exciting feel and mode of development. Track 12 builds to a crescendo. Eventually cutting dead. This is accompanied by a simultaneous blackout.*

The End.

LYRICS

Angel Eyes

The heavens said you wanted me,
But truthfully they lied.
You came to me in prophecy
When hope in me had died.
I doubted you for far too long
I must apologise
I seem reflected
In your burning Angel Eyes.

Don't turn, don't burn, don't turn me with your Angel Eyes.

How can you believe in me,
When the way I carry on, means that
Everything I ever had is gone,
But I'm searchin' and I'm dreamin'
For my fortunes turning tide
When I win more than I lose
To your burning Angel Eyes

Don't turn don't burn me with your Angel Eyes.

Memories all fading fast,
As our love turns to dust
I'm learning that the things I feel,
Are things I just can't trust
Messenger of my fate
On you I must rely
I am transparent to your gaze
I'm blinded by your Angel Eyes.

Don't turn, don't burn me with your Angel Eyes etc.

Track 12

The heavens said you wanted me,
But truthfully they lied.
You came to me in prophecy
When hope in me had died.
I doubted you for far too long
I must apologise
I seem reflected
In your burning Angel Eyes.

How can you believe in me,
When the way I carry on, means that
Everything I ever had is ("Call the police"),
Gone, (gone, gone)
But I'm searchin' and I'm dreamin' ("Home At Last")
For my fortunes turning tide
When I win more than...
To your burning Angel Eyes.

Memories all fading fast,
As your love turns to dust

(Are you nervous, are you hot or cold) this doesn't make
                                        much sense
Failure has taken residence I see, I conquer, I mar
(The ether is my habitat) The way I've lived so far
I want to dance in time with you (to the pixels on the screen)
To dance and rhyme is all I do (that's the message that it
                                        beams)
(But yes is the answer) to the questions that I meet
And (no is the meaning) I must carry in my feet
(No more in feelings will I trust) No more in feelings
                                        will I trust
(My memory now fades to dust) Now watch me disappear
Your future welfare is secure (that's all I want to hear)

Just stop! (I'll stop)
And check (Check mate)

Check mike (Get it right)
So check, check check check check
Sound check, check check check check
Round check, check check check check
Fat cheque, check check check check

This chick just flown the coop
Flying through space looping the loop
She done jumped down from her pedestal
Got a love affair with silicon and metal
Our minds are in ether space
Where love is mathematical regardless of creed and race
But why should this be so
Don't our Gods instruct us as above so below?
Somehow we lost our track
Now all we see is red and yellow pink and black
Tell me who said it should turn out that way
In the future machinery is going to lock that away

It's the digital revolution
We're having digital conversations
We're making digital love relations
And if you don't believe it's true wake up and look
around you

Check check check check check – (the medium)
Check check check – (is the message)
Check check check – (is the meaning of our lives)

Wire is a medium that connects from me to you
But that don't tell me how you are, like live connections do
You're busy trying to join me in that ether time and space
By white lining and bush burning, but that can never
                                        take the place
Of human care and understanding, which is how we
                                        ought to be
So don't mistake the Ethernet for our own telepathy.
Let's stop (We've stopped)
And check (Check what?)

Check check check check check – (the medium/check
sound)
Check check check – (is the message/check round)
Check check check – (is the virus in our lives/Fat cheque)

The only hope for salvation is you and me
Our lives ain't a software no-care program that runs for free
Use our minds to understand the limits of the galaxy
Don't misuse abuse
Reject neglect
Come see conquer mar
Underestimate the complexity
We all reach time to log off and need someone to tell
goodbyes
But machinery is implacable – It ain't got Angel eyes
So stop (Can't stop)

And check (Can't hear you)
Check check check check check – (the problem/check
sound)
Check check check – (is the message/check doubt)
Check check check – (in the virus in our lives/check out)
Just stop!